About Skill Builders Spelling

by Hollie Hendricks

Welcome to RBP Books' Skill Builders series. Like our Summer Bridge Activities collection, the Skill Builders series is designed to make learning both fun and rewarding.

This workbook is based on core curriculum and designed to reinforce classroom spelling skills and strategies for first graders. This workbook holds students' interest with the right mix of challenge, imagination, and instruction. The diverse assignments teach spelling while giving the students something fun to think about—from kissing kangaroos to buried treasure. As students complete the workbook, they will be well prepared to challenge themselves with more difficult words and vocabulary.

A critical thinking section includes exercises to help develop higher-order thinking skills.

Learning is more effective when approached with an element of fun and enthusiasm—just as most children approach life. That's why the Skill Builders combine entertaining and academically sound exercises with eye-catching graphics and fun themes—to make reviewing basic skills at school or home fun and effective, for both you and your budding scholars.

Table of Contents

Beginning Sounds 3–5

Ending Sounds 6–8

Short *a* Words 9–11

Short *o* Words 12–14

Color Words 15–17

Number Words 18–21

Short *e* Words 22–24

Short *i* Words 25–27

Opposites 28–30

Verbs and Nouns 31–33

Short *u* Words 34–36

Blends 37–38

Long *a* Words 39–41

wh 42

th 43

sh 44

ch 45

Long *e* Words 46–48

Alphabetical Order 49–51

Long *i* Words 52–54

Contractions 55–57

Long *o* Words 58–60

Compound Words 61–63

Long *u* Words 64–66

Order Words 67

Critical Thinking Skills
   "X Marks the Spot" 68
   Shipwrecked Short Vowels . 69
   Counting Words Cliff 70
   Long Vowel Lake 71
   Blending Rock 72
   Opposites Island 73
   Contraction Cave 74
   Buried Treasure 75

Answer Pages 76–79

Beginning Sounds

Each silly picture below stands for one letter. Write the <u>beginning letter</u> of the words in each picture.

Example:

a

Beginning Sounds

What letter does your first name start with? Write it below.

_____
- - - - - - - - - - - -
_____

Write eight words you know that begin with that letter.

_____ _____ _____
- -
_____ _____ _____

_____ _____ _____
- -
_____ _____ _____

_____ _____
- -
_____ _____

In the box below draw a picture of yourself and at least three things you listed.

Beginning Sounds

Look around the room or your house and find things that <u>begin</u> with the letters below. Write the name for each thing you find next to the letter it starts with.

Example:

b __books__

c _____   m _____

e _____   n _____

f _____   o _____

g _____   p _____

h _____   r _____

i _____   t _____

j _____   w _____

l _____   y _____

© RBP Books   Spelling Grade 1—RBP0741

Ending Sounds

Each picture below stands for one letter. Write the <u>ending letter</u> of the words in each picture.

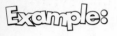 Example:

$$\dagger$$

_____
- - - - - - - -
_____

_____
- - - - - - - -
_____

_____
- - - - - - - -
_____

Ending Sounds

What letter does your favorite color <u>end</u> with?

_____

- - - - - - - - -

_____

Write eight words you know that end with that letter.

_____   _____   _____

- - - - - - - - - -   - - - - - - - - - -   - - - - - - - - - -

_____   _____   _____

_____   _____   _____

- - - - - - - - - -   - - - - - - - - - -   - - - - - - - - - -

_____   _____   _____

_____   _____

- - - - - - - - - -   - - - - - - - - - -

_____   _____

In the box below, use your favorite color to draw at least three of the words you listed in the box.

Look in your kitchen cupboards or fridge. See if you can find a food that <u>ends</u> with each letter listed below.

Example:

a ___banana___

b _____   o _____

c _____   p _____

d _____   r _____

k _____   s _____

l _____   t _____

m _____   w _____

n _____   y _____

Short a Words

pan	man	van	tan
ran	land	fan	hand

Write each word under its picture. Use the words or pictures to make a rhyming "movie" on another sheet of paper. Write one or two sentences that tell what is happening in your "movie" on the lines below. Try to use the **high frequency words** in your sentences.

Example:
The fan **and** the van **can** give the man a hand.

Spelling Grade 1—RBP0741

Short *a* Words

High Frequency Words:

ham	trap	axe	has
as	cap	crab	bad
had	band	apple	after

High Frequency Words:
has,
had,
after, as

Look for these **short *a*** words in the word search. Spell the words you find below their pictures. Look for the **high frequency words,** too, and write them on the last four lines.

```
c r a b m a h g s a h s y k c
a p a r t a f t e r c q h w a
u x p y j l e l p p a h a d p
n v e j d a b f g d n a b b f
```

Example:

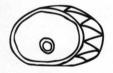 

ham

Short *a* Words

pat	hat	cat	mat
vat	rat	sat	bat

High Frequency Words:
at,
that

Write each word under its picture. Use the words or pictures to make a rhyming "video game" on another sheet of paper. Write one or two sentences that tell what is happening in your "video game" on the lines. Try to use the **high frequency words** in your sentences.

Example:
The cat sat on **that** hat.

_____ _____ _____ _____

_____ _____ _____ _____

Spelling Grade 1—RBP0741

Short *o* Words

top	stop	pop	mop
hop	shop	cop	chop

Write each word under its picture. Use the words or pictures to make a rhyming "T.V. show" on another sheet of paper. Write one or two sentences that tell what is happening in your "T.V. show" on the lines. Try to use the **high frequency words** in your sentences.

Example:

The cop **from** the shop did **not** stop.

Short *o* Words

lock	box	sock	pot
doll	fox	hot	dot

Look for these **short o** words in the word search. Spell the words you find on the lines below their pictures.

```
o  l  o  c  k  h  b  s  m  k  u  j  t
u  d  o  t  k  l  j  u  h  c  f  t  b
g  o  x  o  o  l  m  e  f  o  o  p  r
z  o  z  h  v  o  v  n  p  s  x  m  i
b  n  c  o  e  d  f  w  b  z  k  b  t
w  x  j  q  t  o  q  t  o  p  k  r  j
```

Example:

lock _____ _____ _____

   ●

_____ _____ _____ _____

Short *o* Words

frog	dog	clog	log
fog	cog	hog	jog

Write each word under its picture. Use the words or pictures to make a rhyming "postcard" on another sheet of paper. Write one or two sentences that tell what is happening in your "postcard" on the lines. Try to use the **high frequency words** in your sentences.

Example:

The frog took a **long** jog in the fog.

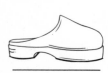

Color Words

red	green	pink	white	orange
blue	brown	yellow	purple	black

Color the picture below using the colors that match the words.

Copy each word on the lines below.

Example:

orange orange   pink _____

yellow _____   blue _____

green _____   black _____

brown _____   red _____

purple _____   white _____

Spelling Grade 1—RBP0741

Color Words

red	green	pink	white	orange
blue	brown	yellow	purple	black

Look out the window, and write down the colors you see for each object pictured below.

Example:

trees

_____ green and brown

flowers

_____ and _____

houses

_____ and _____

cars

_____ and _____

www.summerbridgeactivities.com

Color Words

red	green	pink	white	orange
blue	brown	yellow	purple	black

Write something you know about each color on the lines below. Be sure to write in complete sentences and use a capital at the beginning and a period at the end.

Example:

red   Apples can be red.

orange _____

yellow _____

green _____

blue _____

purple _____

pink _____

brown _____

17

Number Words

High Frequency Words:
one
two

~~one~~ four seven ten
two five eight eleven
three six nine twelve

Match the number word with its picture.

Example:

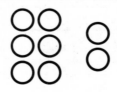

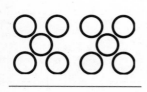

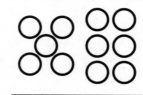

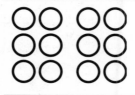

Number Words

one	four	seven	ten
two	five	eight	eleven
three	six	nine	twelve

Look at your room. Tell how many things you see of each number. Write in complete sentences with a capital at the beginning and a period at the end. Underline the number word in your sentence.

Example:

one   <u></u>I see <u>one</u> window.
    capital   period

two

three

four

five

six

19

Number Words

one	four	seven	ten
two	five	eight	eleven
three	six	nine	twelve

Look at your room. Tell how many things you see of each number. Write in complete sentences with a capital at the beginning and a period at the end. Underline the number word in your sentence.

Example:

seven   I see seven birds.
        capital   period

eight   _____

nine   _____

ten   _____

eleven   _____

twelve   _____

Number Words

1—first	6—sixth
2—second	7—seventh
3—third	8—eighth
4—fourth	9—ninth
5—fifth	10—tenth

High Frequency Words: *first*

Put the steps in order for making a peanut butter sandwich by writing the correct number next to each step.

10 Take a bite! Yum!

_____ Open the peanut butter and jelly.

_____ Find some peanut butter and jelly.

_____ Hold the sandwich.

_____ Get two pieces of bread. Spread the first with peanut butter.

_____ Slice the sandwich in half.

_____ Spread the second with jelly.

_____ Put each half on a plate.

_____ Sit down with a glass of milk and your sandwich on a plate.

_____ Put the slices of bread together to make a sandwich.

Spelling Grade 1—RBP0741

Short e Words

tend	send	mend	pen
ten	den	hen	men

Write each word under its picture. Use the words or pictures to make a rhyming "cartoon" on another sheet of paper. Write one or two sentences that tell what is happening in your "cartoon" on the lines. Try to use the **high frequency words** in your sentences.

Example:

When the hen got the pen she drew a ten.

Short e Words

nest	yes	best	web
well	bell	bed	leg

Look for these **short e** words in the word search. Spell the words you find on the lines below their pictures.

```
t  t  g  r  l  k  v  t  a  w  d  x  k
s  o  s  n  l  l  e  b  x  l  y  p  e
s  u  l  e  s  b  e  w  e  v  e  l  m
p  h  a  f  n  v  b  g  o  s  e  y  k
t  w  e  l  l  e  d  x  v  k  q  f  n
b  l  b  t  d  r  b  e  s  t  z  m  j
```

Example:

nest _____ _____ _____

_____ _____ yes _____

23

Short e Words

net   set   jet   get
pet   met   fret   wet

Write each word under its picture. Use the words or pictures to make a rhyming "story" on another sheet of paper. Write one or two sentences that tell what is happening in your "story" on the lines. Try to use the **high frequency words** in your sentences.

Example:

The pet set the **very** wet net on **them**.

_____   _____   _____   _____

- - - - - -   - - - - - -   - - - - - -   - - - - - -

_____   _____   _____   _____

- - - - - -   - - - - - -   - - - - - -   - - - - - -

_____

_____

_____

Short *i* Words

win	chin	pin
bin	fin	tin

You are taking pictures of the rhyming *-in* family at their reunion. Write each word under its picture. Use the words or pictures to make a "photo" on another sheet of paper. Write one or two sentences that tell what is happening in your "photo" on the lines below. Try to use the **high frequency words** in your sentences.

Example:

Did she win that pin?

---- ---- ---- ----

---- ---- ---- ----

---- ---- ---- ----

---- ---- ---- ----

---- ---- ---- ----

---- ---- ---- ----

---- ---- ---- ---- ---- ---- ---- ---- ---- ---- ----

---- ---- ---- ---- ---- ---- ---- ---- ---- ---- ----

Spelling Grade 1—RBP0741

Short *i* Words

his, this, if, will

hill   dill   bill
fill   pill   gill

There is a picture in the news about the *-ill* bunch. Write each word under its picture. Use the words or pictures to make a "photo" on another sheet of paper. Be a reporter and write one or two sentences that tell what is happening on the lines below. Try to use the **high frequency words** in your sentences.

Example:

Will his gill get well with a pill?

_____

- - - - - - - - - - - -

_____

_____

- - - - - - - - - - - -

_____

_____

- - - - - - - - - - - -

_____

_____

- - - - - - - - - - - -

_____

_____

- - - - - - - - - - - -

_____

_____

- - - - - - - - - - - -

_____

_____

- -

_____

- -

Short *i* Words

Draw lines to connect the numbered dots in order, but make sure you only connect **short *i*** words.

High Frequency Words: *into, him, its*

For example, put your pencil on the number 1 dot. *Into* is a short *i* word. Read the number 2 word. *Tack* is not a short *i* word. Skip to number 3. *Still* is a short *i* word. Draw a line from number 1 to number 3.

When you have connected all the short *i* dots, write the name of the picture you drew at the bottom of the page.

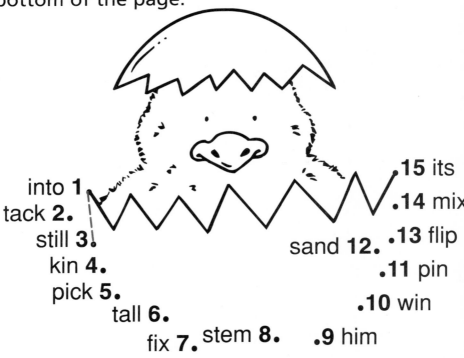

into **1**
tack **2.**
still **3.**
kin **4.**
pick **5.**
tall **6.**
fix **7.** stem **8.**
sand **12.**
15 its
.14 mix
.13 flip
.11 pin
.10 win
.9 him

Spelling Grade 1—RBP0741

Opposites

High Frequency Words: *in, down, up, out, little*

in	out	up
down	big	little

For each number, choose one of the opposite words and circle it. Write a sentence using the word you circled.

Example:

down / (up):

I wake up in the morning.

1. in / out:

_____

_____

_____

_____

2. big / little:

_____

_____

_____

_____

28

Opposites

short   tall   fat
thin   hard   soft

Walk around the house or room and write the name of something that fits each group of opposites.

Example:

short *garbage can*

1. tall

2. fat

3. thin

4. hard

5. soft

Opposites

yummy   sharp   sweet
eat   sticky   dry

Fix the silly story by changing all of the underlined words into the opposites from the list above.

_____

Today I helped Mom make a <u>yucky</u> _____

_____

snack. Mom took a <u>dull</u> _____ knife and

_____

sliced some <u>sour</u> _____ oranges for me

_____

to <u>drink</u> _____. My hands were <u>clean</u>

_____

_____ from eating the juicy oranges. I

washed them and rubbed them with a <u>wet</u>

_____

_____ towel. Thanks, Mom!

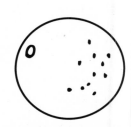

Naming words are <u>nouns</u>:
  boy   girl   cat

Action words are <u>verbs</u>:
  stand   ~~dance~~   fall   fly   ride   hug

Write the correct naming word, or <u>noun</u>, below its picture. Then ask each noun a question. Use an action word, or <u>verb</u>, in your sentence. Use the words on this page.

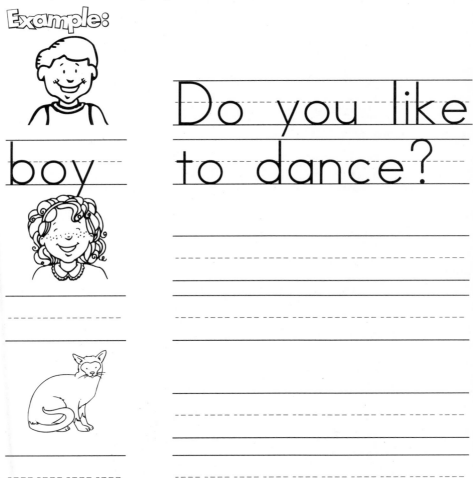

Example:

boy

Do you like to dance?

31

Verbs and Nouns

nouns:
  dog   man   bird

verbs:
  jump   run   sleep
  walk   hop   sit

Make a silly story by putting any nouns and verbs you choose on the lines below. Use each noun and verb only one time in the story.

_____   _____

A _____ wanted to _____.
      noun   verb

_____   _____

But the _____ wanted to _____.
       noun   verb

_____   _____

And the _____ tried to _____.
       noun   verb

At last, so everyone could be happy, they all

_____

agreed to _____.
     verb

Verbs and Nouns

nouns:

frog   fish   bee

verbs:

eat   bake   swim

draw   yell   smile

Write a play (a story you can act out) using the nouns and verbs above. You can use some **high frequency words** from other pages, too.

Short *u* Words

fun   stun   bun
sun   run   crunch

Imagine that you are watching a baseball game. Write each word under its matching picture. Draw a baseball diamond on a separate sheet of paper. Use the words or pictures to show what might happen. Write one or two sentences that tell about it. Try to use the **high frequency words** in your sentences.

_____   _____   _____

_____   _____   _____

_____

_____

_____

Short *u* Words

rug   dug   tug
hug   bug   jug

The neighbor's dog was just in your yard. Write each word under its matching picture. Use the words or pictures to tell what may have happened in your yard. Write one or two sentences that tell what is happening. Try to use the **high frequency words** in your sentences.

Short *u* Words

Draw lines to connect the numbered dots in order, but make sure you only connect **short *u*** words.

For example, put your pencil on the number 1 dot. *Up* is a short *u* word. Read the number 2 word: *tin* is not a short *u* word. Skip to the next number. Dot number 3, *duck*, is a short *u* word. Draw a line from number 1 to number 3.

When you have connected all the short *u* dots, write the name of the picture you drew at the bottom of the page.

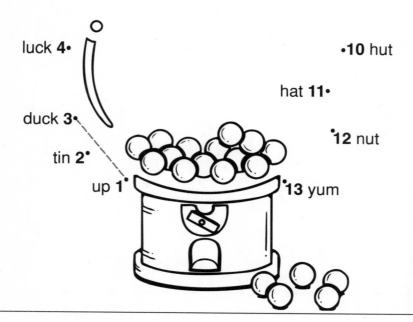

mud **7**

.8 mad

cut **5.**   **•6** ask   **.9** cup

luck **4•**   **•10** hut

hat **11•**

duck **3•**   **•12** nut

tin **2•**

up **1•**   **•13** yum

Blends

Fill in the correct blend to finish each word.

fr__og

1. _____ own   **2.** _____ ince

3. _____ ess   **4.** _____ apes

5.  _____ ain   **6.** _____ ick

Spelling Grade 1—RBP0741

Fill in the correct blend to finish each word.

Example:

c|own

1. _____ ate

2. _____ eep

3. _____ ocks

4. _____ ower

5. _____ ue

6. _____ ock

Long *a* Words

cake	tape	race
flame	base	late

High Frequency Words: *make, made*

Write each word under its matching picture. Use the words or pictures to make a "movie" on another sheet of paper. Write one or two sentences that tell what is happening in your "movie." Try to use the **high frequency words** in your sentences.

Example:

The race to **make** a cake started late.

_____

- - - - - - - - - -

_____

_____

- - - - - - - - - -

_____

_____

- - - - - - - - - -

_____

_____

- - - - - - - - - -

_____

_____

- - - - - - - - - -

_____

_____

- - - - - - - - - -

_____

_____

- -

_____

_____

- -

_____

Long *a* Words

High Frequency Words:

are,

was,

the, or

rain   stain   trail

sail   plain   wait

Write each word under its matching picture. Use the words or pictures to make a rhyming "video game" on another sheet of paper. Write one or two sentences that tell what is happening in your "video game." Try to use the **high frequency words** in your sentences.

Example:

There **was** rain on **the** trail in **the** plain.

_____

_____

_____

_____

_____

_____

Plain Yogurt

_____

_____

_____

_____

_____

_____

_____

_____

_____

_____

_____

Long *a* Words

play	hay	jay	lay
stay	bay	day	clay

Look for these **long *a*** words in the word search. Spell the words you find on the lines below their pictures. Look for the **high frequency words,** too, and write them on the last four lines.

High Frequency Words:
way, may, all, by

y	a	w	y	a	l	m	t	l	b	c	f	l	n	b	m
x	y	b	y	y	a	l	c	w	z	d	l	z	l	a	l
n	p	y	a	l	p	f	c	w	t	a	u	a	y	v	e
y	a	d	b	l	s	t	a	y	z	v	w	b	o	y	y
s	a	o	p	w	n	h	y	a	b	e	n	d	q	v	a
t	h	h	w	m	v	g	u	a	a	n	g	e	w	y	j

Example:

p l a y

_____ _____ _____

_____ _____ _____ _____

_____ _____ _____ _____

_____ _____ _____ _____

41

wh

High Frequency Words:

where, what

whistle   white   whip
wheel   whale   while

Tell what you see in this silly picture on the lines below. Try to use the **high frequency words.**

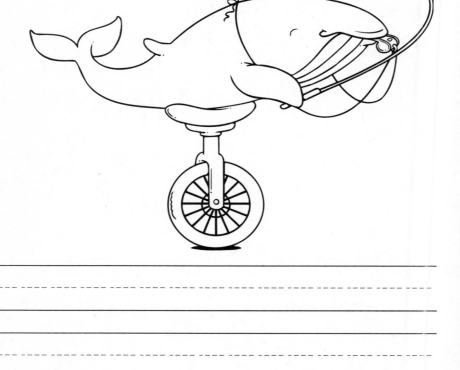

_____

_____

_____

_____

_____

_____

_____

_____

th

thick   path   thin
three   bath   thorn

Tell what you see in this silly picture on the lines below. Try to use the **high frequency words.**

_____

_____

_____

_____

_____

_____

_____

Spelling Grade 1—RBP0741

sh

ship   shark   shell
washes   shines   shore

Tell what you see in this silly picture on the lines below. Try to use the high frequency word.

-----

ch

cheese   cheep   chick
cherries   chase   children

Write each word under its matching picture. Use these words to write a silly sentence on the lines below. Then draw a picture of it. Try to use the **high frequency words.**

High Frequency Words:
each, which

_____

_____

_____

_____

_____

_____

_____

_____

_____

    Spelling Grade 1—RBP0741

Long e Words

bee   need   weed
tree   seed   peel

Write each word under its matching picture. Use the words or pictures to make a rhyming "cartoon" on another sheet of paper. Write one or two sentences that tell what is happening in your "cartoon" on the lines below. Try to use the **high frequency words** in your sentences.

Example:

I can **see** a bee in that tree.

Long e Words

eat	read	clean
seat	cream	steam

Write each word under its matching picture. Use the words or pictures to make a rhyming "story" on another sheet of paper. Write one or two sentences that tell what is happening in your "story" on the lines below. Try to use the **high frequency words** in your sentences.

Example:

Some **people** like to eat ice cream.

_____

_____

_____

_____

_____

_____

_____

_____

_____

_____

Long e Words

Look for these **long e** words in the word search. Spell the words you find on the lines below their pictures.

meat	sheep	sleep	heat
leap	leak	between	seen

```
c p u f s x s y c q e h e a t o
y t o m l l h n q c v q m e a t
t k w l e z e y u z h z h d s p
n q a e e j e d i l l t p e e s
i j f a p x p m l b e t w e e n
q s b p t p y k l l e a k w n t
```

Example:

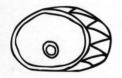  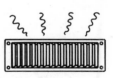

meat _____ _____ _____

_____ _____ _____ _____

Alphabetical Order

Write the first names of up to five people in your family in the first column. Rewrite the names in ABC order in the second column. Draw a picture of the family members you named.

a
b
c
d
e
f
g
h
i
j
k
l
m
n
o
p
q
r
s
t
u
v
w
x
y
z

Alphabetical Order

a b c d e f g h i j k l m n o p q r s t u v w x y z

Choose seven of your favorite toys or games. Line them up in alphabetical order. Write their names in ABC order on the lines below.

_____

_____

_____

_____

_____

_____

_____

Alphabetical Order

Write the names of six animals you might find at the zoo. Draw a line to the number that shows where that animal's name would be in ABC order.

1.

2.

3.

4.

5.

6.

a
b
c
d
e
f
g
h
i
j
k
l
m
n
o
p
q
r
s
t
u
v
w
x
y
z

Long *i* Words

High Frequency Words:

like,
time

kite   tie   bite
bike   wipe   dive

Write each word under its picture. Use the words or pictures to make a "photo" about the **long *i*** family on another sheet of paper. Write one or two sentences that tell what is happening on the lines. Try to use the **high frequency words**.

Example:

They **like** to bike in ties.

52

Long *i* Words

kind   wind   mind
rind   behind   bind

Imagine you are taking pictures of the rhyming *-ind* family. Write each word below its picture. Use the words to make a "photo" on another sheet of paper. Write one or two sentences that tell what is happening in your "photo" on the lines. Try to use the **high frequency words**.

Example:

I find that this family is kind.

_____

_____

_____

_____

_____

_____

_____

_____

_____

_____

_____

_____

_____

_____

_____

_____

Spelling Grade 1—RBP0741

Long *i* Words

Draw lines to connect the numbered dots in order, but make sure you only connect **long *i*** words. For example, put your pencil on the number 1 dot. *Pine* is a long *i* word. Read the number 2 word. *Hit* is not a long *i* word. Skip to number 3. *Nine* is a long *i* word. Draw a line from number 1 to number 3. When you have connected all the long *i* dots, write the name of the picture you drew at the bottom of the page.

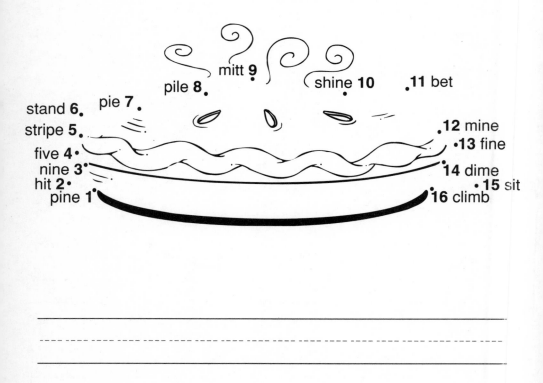

stand 6.
pie 7.
mitt 9
pile 8.
shine 10
.11 bet
stripe 5.
.12 mine
five 4•
•13 fine
nine 3•
14 dime
hit 2•
• 15 sit
pine 1•
16 climb

www.summerbridgeactivities.com   ©RBP Books

Contractions

won't   aren't   don't

You are at the amusement park on the Contraction Bumper Cars. Write the new contraction each pair of cars makes when they crash together.

High Frequency Words: *do*

1.

2.

3.

Spelling Grade 1—RBP0741

Contractions

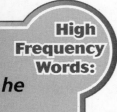
they're   I'm   we're
I'll   she'll   he'll

Make roller coaster loops that connect each contraction to the words it is made of.

Example:

I'm

I - - - - - - - am

will

they're

he'll

they   are

he

I

we

I'll

we're

are   will

she'll

she   will

© RBP Books

Contractions

that's   it's   we'll

Play a game of "Contraction Miniature Golf." Connect each club to a ball. Write the contraction they make on the line.

 that

is

_____

 it

is

we

will

Long *o* Words

High Frequency Words: *so, no, only, more*

stove   hole   home
yoke   core   rope

Write each word below its picture. Use the words or pictures to make up a "T.V. show" on another sheet of paper. Write one or two sentences that tell what is happening in your "T.V. show" on the lines. Try to use the **high frequency words**.

Example:

We have **no** stove at home.

Long *o* Words

coat   bow   boat
go   crow   old

High Frequency Words:
most, know, over

Write each word below its picture. Use the words or pictures to make a "postcard" on another sheet of paper. Write one or two sentences that tell what is happening on your "postcard" on the lines. Try to use the **high frequency words**.

Example:

A crow can go **over** the boat.

Spelling Grade 1—RBP0741

Long *o* Words

Look for these **long o** words in the word search. Spell the words you find on the lines under their pictures.

open	door	soap	poor
oats	shore	floor	roll

```
x m l k b e n a y p b f p r v n
r b i p o o j q r o o n o x y k
q o a d d o o r r r p o n v n i
v o l e m s o a t s l e r o i y
s g o l k d j s q f q x n m p w
p s h o r e l q j h h u a j n v
```

Example:

open _____ _____ _____

  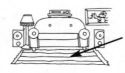 

_____ _____ _____ _____

Compound Words

snowflake   fireplace
butterfly   spaceship

Match the compound word with its definition. Write a sentence using a **high frequency word** and one compound word from this page on the lines.

Example:

snowflake   a frozen raindrop falling from the sky

_____   a flying insect

_____   a place to build a fire

_____   a ship that goes into space

_____

_____

© RBP Books   Spelling Grade 1—RBP0741

Compound Words

birthday   raindrop   notebook

Write a definition for each compound word. Use the correct **high frequency word** in the definition it belongs to.

Example:

birthday

the day of your birth

raindrop

_____

_____

_____

notebook

_____

_____

_____

62

Compound Words

mailbox   seashore   seashells

Fill in the missing words from the story. Use the compound words and the **high frequency words.**

High Frequency Words: *called, many, her, my, who*

Example:

My favorite thing to do is to collect

_____

_____ on the

_____

_____, Grandma likes to call and

_____

ask how _____ I collected. Today, I put a package of

_____

my seashells in the _____,

_____

_____ do you think they were for?

_____

Yes, they were for _____ grandma!

Long *u* Words

use, a, were, would

fuse   flute   huge
mule   cute   blue

Imagine that you are a reporter watching a Fourth of July parade. Write each word below its matching picture. Use the words to write one or two sentences that tell what you might see. Try to use the **high frequency words** in your sentences.

Long *u* Words

fruit   suit   balloon
raccoon   pool   tool

When you got up this morning and looked out the window, you saw a strange sight! Write each word below its matching picture. Use the words to write one or two sentences that tell what you saw. Try to use the **high frequency words** in your sentences.

High Frequency Words:
have,
your,
their,
could

        Spelling Grade 1—RBP0741

Long *u* Words

stew   crew   new
blew   flew   dew

Write each word below its matching picture. Use the words or pictures to make a rhyming "story" on another sheet of paper. Write one or two sentences that tell what is happening in your story on the lines. Try to use the **high frequency words**.

Example:

How did the crew make the stew?

66

Order Words

before   after   first   last   middle

Animals are standing in line to see *The Zany Zoo* movie at the theater. Use the order words listed above to tell where the animals are standing in line.

Example:

1. The mouse is <u>before</u> the giraffe.

2. The hippo is _____ the zebra.

3. The zebra is _____ in line.

4. The giraffe is _____ in line.

5. The beaver is in the _____.

Spelling Grade 1—RBP0741

"X Marks the Spot" Treasure Hunt

The treasure map below shows the path you must take to find the treasure. (You will need the answers from pages 69–75 to find out what the treasure is!)

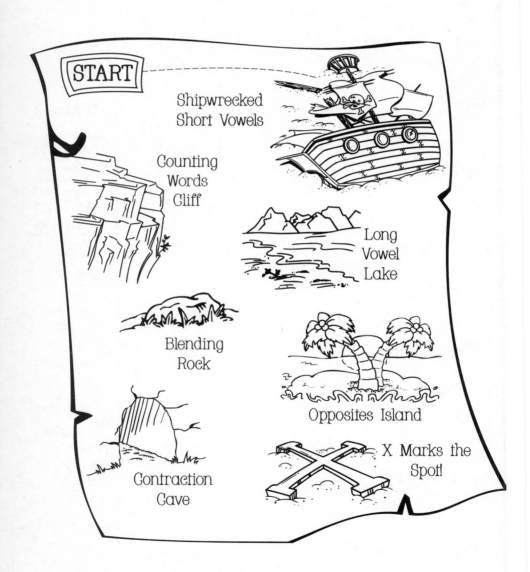

START

Shipwrecked Short Vowels

Counting Words Cliff

Long Vowel Lake

Blending Rock

Opposites Island

Contraction Cave

X Marks the Spot!

Shipwrecked Short Vowels

The short vowel words on the shipwreck below are misspelled. Fix the words to get you closer to the treasure!

nit

cin

hot

rag

shop

pat

Spelling Grade 1—RBP0741

Counting Words Cliff

Write the number or number word on each line of the cliff as you follow them to the top.

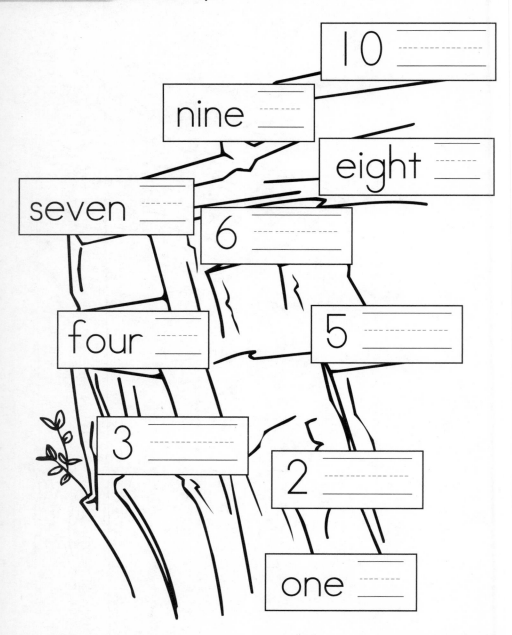

Long Vowel Lake

Write the word for each object lost at the bottom of the lake.

Spelling Grade 1—RBP0741

Blending Rock

Write the word or draw a picture that matches each item you see on Blending Rock.

sky

flower

tree

Opposites Island

front   back   on
open   off   closed

On each side of the island the animals are doing the opposite of those on the other side. Write the opposite action you see by the pictures.

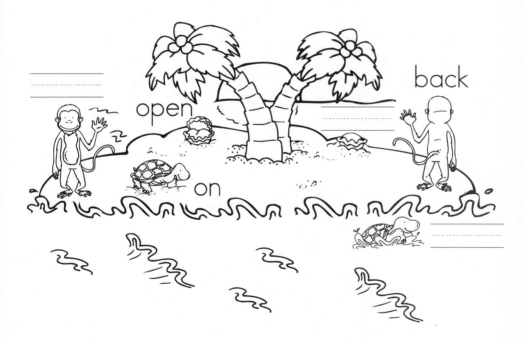

open

back

on

73

Contraction Cave

This cave has hanging contractions that are falling and breaking apart into words on the floor below. Write the two words each contraction makes after it falls.

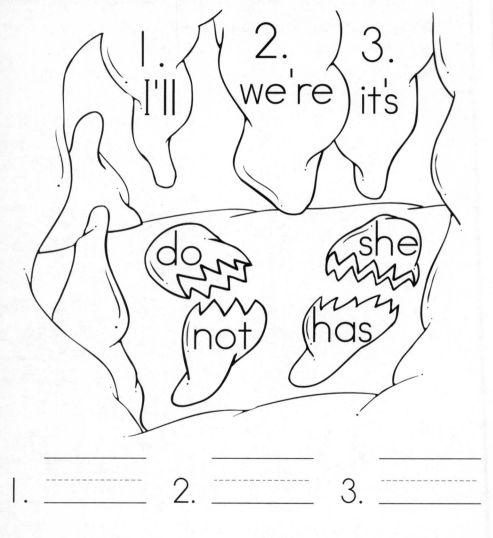

1. _____ _____

2. _____ _____

3. _____ _____

Buried Treasure

Great work! You've found the X and the hidden treasure box! To find out what is inside you will need to look at each page you did and collect the clues to see the treasure.

Critical Thinking Skills

1. "Shipwrecked Short Vowels"—What can you can lay on the floor and sit on? I am the last letter of this word.

2. "Counting Words Cliff"—What number do you start with when counting? I am the first letter in this word.

3. "Long Vowel Lake"—What can you eat food from? I am the second letter in this word.

4. "Blending Rock"—What can you ride on when it snows? I am the fourth letter in this word.

5. "Opposites Island"—What word means the opposite of "back?" I am the beginning letter in this word.

6. "Contraction Cave"—What word on this page has only one letter and means "me?" I am the only letter in this word.

1 2 3 4 5 6 7 8

*Hint: The treasure is a compound word. To find the last letters solve this riddle: What should you do with your hands before you eat?

___ ___ ___ ___
7   8

Spelling Grade 1—RBP0741

Answer Pages

Page 3
a, d, s, k

Page 4
Answers will vary.

Page 5
Answers will vary.

Page 6
t, x, n, r

Page 7
Answers will vary.

Page 8
Answers will vary.

Page 9
fan, tan, ran, man
pan, hand, land, van

Page 10

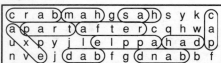

ham, apple, crab, axe
bad, cap, band, trap

Page 11
cat, mat, vat, bat
hat, pat, rat, lap

Page 12
pop, top, cop, mop
shop, chop, stop, hop

Page 13

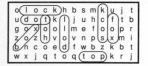

lock, hot, doll, box
sock, fox, pot, dot

Page 14
cog, fog, jog, hog
dog, clog, frog, log

Page 15
orange, pink, yellow, blue, green,
black, brown, red, purple, white

Page 16
Answers will vary.

Page 17
Answers will vary.

Page 18
one, two three
four, five, six
seven, eight, nine
ten, eleven, twelve

Page 19
Answers will vary.

Page 20
Answers will vary.

Page 21
10, 2, 1, 9, 3, 6, 4, 7, 8, 5

Page 22
mend, pen, men, ten
send, tend, hen, den

Page 23

nest, web, best, leg
well, bell, yes, bed

Answer Pages

Page 24
net, fret, get, met
set, jet, wet, pet

Page 25
chin, tin, bin
fin, win, pin

Page 26
hill, dill, fill
bill, gill, pill

Page 27

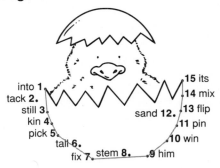

into 1
tack 2.
still 3.
kin 4.
pick 5.
tall 6.
fix 7. stem 8. 9 him
sand 12. 13 flip
11 pin
10 win
15 its
14 mix

egg hatching

Page 28
Answers will vary.

Page 29
Answers will vary.

Page 30
yummy, sharp, sweet, eat, sticky, dry

Page 31
boy, girl, cat
Sentences will vary.

Page 32
Answers will vary.

Page 33
Answers will vary.

Page 34
run, sun, stun
bun, crunch, fun

Page 35
dug, rug, tug, hug, bug, jug

Page 36

mud 7   8 mad
cut 5   6 ask   9 cup
luck 4   10 hut
hat 11
duck 3   12 nut
tin 2
up 1   13 yum

gumball machine

Page 37
1. crown
2. prince
3. dress
4. grapes
5. train
6. brick

Page 38
1. plate
2. sleep
3. blocks
4. flower
5. glue
6. clock

Page 39
cake, race, late
flame, base, tape

Page 40
trail, sail, wait
plain, stain, rain

Answer Pages

Page 41

```
y a w y a l m t l b c f l n b m
x y b y y a l c w z d l z l a l
n p y a l p f c w t a u a y v e
y a d b l s t a y z v w b o y y
s a o p w n h y a b e n d q v a
t h h w m v g u a a n g e w y j
```

play, jay, hay, clay
lay, stay, bay, day

Page 42
A white whale is blowing a whistle while whipping on a wheel.

Page 43
These thick thorns grow there on a path around the three birds on the bath.

Page 44
A shark washes a shell ship while the sun shines on the shore.

Page 45
cheep, cheese, children
chick, cherries, chase

Page 46
bee, need, weed
tree, seed, peel

Page 47
eat, seat, read
cream, clean, steam

Page 48

```
c p u f s x s y c q e h e a t o
y t o m l l h n q c v q m e a t
t k w l e z e y u z h z h d s p
n q a e e j e d i l l t p e e s
i j f a p x p m l b e t w e e n
q s b p t p y k l l e a k w n t
```

meat, sheep, sleep, heat
leap, leak, between, seen

Page 49
Answers will vary.

Page 50
Answers will vary.

Page 51
Answers will vary.

Page 52
kite, tie, bite
bike, wipe, dive

Page 53
kind, wind, mind
rind, behind, bind

Page 54

pie

Page 55
1. won't
2. aren't
3. don't

Page 56

they're — they
I'm — I am
will — he'll — he
we — we're — are
I — I'll — will
she'll — she will

Answer Pages

Page 57
that's, it's, we'll

Page 58
stove, hole, home
yoke, core, rope

Page 59
coat, bow, boat
go, crow, old

Page 60

```
x m l k b e n a y p b f p r v n
r b i p o o j q r o o n o x y k
q o a d d o o r r p o n v n i
v o l e m s o a t s x e r o i y
s g o l k d j s q f q x n m p w
p s h o r e l q j h h u a j n v
```

open, door, soap, poor
oats, shore, floor, roll

Page 61
snowflake, butterfly, fireplace,
spaceship

Page 62
the day of your birth
a drop of rain
a book to write notes in

Page 63
seashells
seashore
many
mailbox
Who
my

Page 64
fuse, flute, huge
mule, cute, blue

Page 65
fruit, suit, balloon
raccoon, pool, tool

Page 66
stew, crew, new
blew, flew, dew

Page 67
1. before
2. after
3. first
4. last
5. middle

Page 69
hat, net, pot
rug, can, ship

Page 70
1, two, three, 4, five
six, 7, 8, 9, ten

Page 71
plate, bike, rope, flute, peel

Page 72
sled, crab, glove
pictures of tree, flower, sky

Page 73
front, closed, off

Page 74
1. I will
2. we are
3. it is

Page 75
1. rug, g
2. one, o
3. plate, l
4. sled, d
5. front, f
6. I, i
7. s
8. h
Answer to riddle: wash
Buried treasure: goldfish

79

Notes

5 Five things I'm thankful for: